To Rem and Liam, my vital resources of love and support. —J. H.

To the ones who notice, relish, and care for the little details, the tiny pieces from which our whole world is made. If you look closely enough, we are all one. —E. M.

The author would like to thank Douglas G. Capone, PhD, William and Julie Wrigley Chair in Environmental Studies and Professor of Biological Sciences, Wrigley Institute for Environmental Studies, University of Southern California, and Joseph M. Prospero, PhD, Professor Emeritus, Department of Atmospheric Sciences, Rosenstiel School, University of Miami, for reviewing technical sections of this manuscript. Any remaining errors or inconsistencies are my own.

Text copyright © 2023 by Jilanne Hoffmann.
Illustrations copyright © 2023 by Eugenia Mello.

Image Credits

Pages 40–42: NASA's Goddard Space Flight Center. Page 43: Illustration based on NASA image. Page 44: Illustration based on image from *This Dynamic Earth: The Story of Plate Tectonics* (U.S. Geological Survey, 1996). Page 45: Illustration based on image from "Alfred Wegener: Building a Case for Continental Drift," December 7, 2014, https://publish.illinois.edu/alfredwegener/.

Library of Congress Cataloging-in-Publication Data available.

ISBN 978-1-7972-1175-6

Manufactured in China.

Design by Mariam Quraishi and Jennifer Tolo Pierce.
Typeset in ITC Clearface Pro and Binner D.
The illustrations in this book were created digitally.

10 9 8 7 6 5 4 3 2 1

Chronicle Books LLC
680 Second Street
San Francisco, California 94107

Chronicle Books—we see things differently. Become part of our community at www.chroniclekids.com.

The Life-Giving Link
Between North Africa and
the Amazon

of *Dust*

By **Jilanne Hoffmann** *Illustrated by* **Eugenia Mello**

chronicle books · san francisco

Millions of years ago,
no ocean lay between us.

You and I were one.

And then slowly,

slowly,

great forces tore us apart,

creating seven continents

surrounded by vast oceans.

But I've found a way to reach you,   to sustain you,

to help you flourish.

I am dust, the dust of North Africa.

Not just any dust, though.

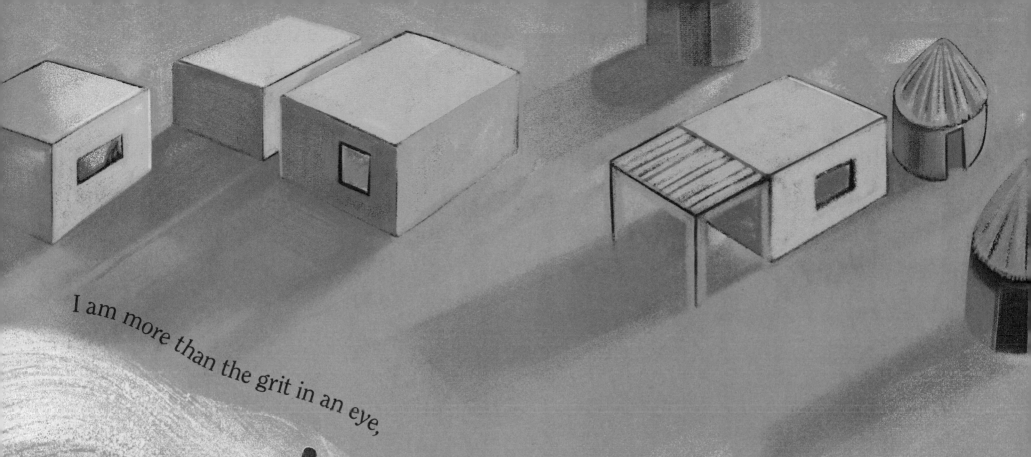

I am more than the grit in an eye,

the smudge on a finger,

the grime that swirls down a drain.

For I connect continents.

I come from the Sahel,
a ribbon of land spread between
the Sahara Desert, to the north,
and the tropical savanna,
to the south.

Land that stretches from the Red Sea, in the east,
to the Atlantic Ocean, in the west.

When the harmattan wind howls across the Sahel,

I begin my journey westward.

What do I carry?

Precious cargo

needed by all life on Earth:

plants, trees,

and animals—

including humans.

I rise in dense, whirling clouds.

I soar above acacia trees

and scrubby, dried tufts of cram-cram grass.

I whip across grasslands

and through bulbous baobab trees.

I shroud the sun, sift through cracks around windows and doors and into eyes and

ears and mouths.

I fly above a river that bends

like an elbow,

tracing a tree and grass oasis

through a desert of rock and sand below.
The air so dry, it cracks the trunks of trees.

I spiral over plateaus of rock as flat as a palm

toward a thick trunk of water

with curving fingers like a hand,

the surrounding land a rich, emerald green.

After a journey of thousands of miles,
I reach the Atlantic Ocean, which rises up,
swirls and foams, then stretches out to meet the sky.

But I have no time
to rest at the shore;
although bits of me scatter groundward,
I still have far to travel.

For I connect continents.

I fly across the Atlantic,
    losing much of myself
        to the restless waves below.

Falling into a dolphin's eye,
    a whale's mouth.
        Perhaps floating forever,
        mixing with the salt
        and krill and seaweed,
            building up the ocean's soup.

Bountiful, boundless,
and purpose-filled,
even in my loss,

I maintain my course.

I fly and fly and fly,
spilling and thinning as I go,
finally reaching you—

a land where clouds and rainfall
   often mask the sun.

A land that blooms and thrives,
that's lush with trees and vines.

I, the dust of Africa,
fall onto your thick canopy
and then onto the earth that anchors your trees—
the Amazon rainforest.

I end my journey here, with you,

renewing our connection.

I release my cargo, phosphorus,
knowing that your rain-washed, depleted soil
could not nourish your trees—

numbering more than
the stars of the Milky Way—

without this vital resource.

And as you flourish, know that I have not forgotten you,

and I hope that you have not forgotten me,

no matter how long we've been apart.

When I reach you, we become one

once again.

Questions for Curious Minds

How did dust help scientists solve the mystery of the Amazon's lush rainforest?

For years, people thought that the Amazon's soil was nutrient-packed because the forest was so lush. Scientists began questioning this belief in the early 1950s, when data suggested that much of the Amazon actually contained depleted soil. Later studies have confirmed that minerals and other nutrients from dead plant matter are quickly absorbed by the roots of plants or are washed away by frequent rains. So what replaces those minerals?

One part of the answer lies within the African continent—thousands of miles east of the Amazon, across the Atlantic Ocean. In 1966, a scientist named Joseph Prospero began measuring airborne dust on the island of Barbados, in the Caribbean. While he was the first to identify the seasonal movement of African dust across the Atlantic, he had no idea how much dust made the trip.

Today, scientists can track dust movement from space and estimate the amount that's airborne. NASA's satellite imagery shows that millions of tons of dust come from the Bodélé Depression, part of an ancient lake bed in Chad. The depression lies within a strip of land called the Sahel on the southern edge of the Sahara Desert. When the winter harmattan wind swirls its way from northeast Africa westward across the Sahel, the dust from the depression begins to fly and mix with that of the Sahara. A 5,000-mile (8,050-kilometre) river of dust in the atmosphere then courses its way across West Africa and the Atlantic Ocean. The bulk of the dust lands in the ocean, but the remaining portion falls mostly on South America. Although amounts and estimates vary widely from year to year, one study suggests that an average of 182 million tons (165 million metric tons) of dust, or about 700,000 18-wheelers' worth, leave the Sahara annually. About 15 percent reaches the Amazon basin. During the summer months, the river of dust shifts northward, falling on the Caribbean and North America.

For much of the Amazon, the dust provides a variety of mineral elements—including phosphorus and iron, which plants need for photosynthesis and seed production. Both are in short supply in the Amazon basin, but phosphorus is particularly scarce.

Dust rises on the harmattan wind, beginning its journey in the Sahel.

An estimated 24,200 tons (21,950 metric tons) of phosphorus carried by dust land in the Amazon basin each year, nearly equaling the amount that scientists think leaches from the soil due to rain. Surprisingly, scientists have also found that much of the phosphorus and iron that fall from above may never reach the ground. Instead, they believe nutrients may be absorbed by the leaves of the trees and plants that live in the rainforest canopy. Just imagine absorbing most of your daily vitamins and minerals through your skin!

Much has been learned since the 1950s, but there is still far more to understand about African dust and its effects on the Amazon rainforest, as well as how climate change may influence all parts of our global ecosystem.

How does dust from the Sahel affect Atlantic Ocean ecosystems?

About 85 percent of the dust that leaves North Africa falls into the Atlantic Ocean. In some parts of the Atlantic, such as the deep ocean far from the shore, both the phosphorus and the iron carried by the dust are in short supply. But of the two, iron is scarcer. One scientist recently calculated that 240 gallons (910 litres) of seawater may contain only one eyelash's weight in iron.

But that tiny amount can make a huge difference. Without it, trillions of microscopic plants called phytoplankton (also known as microalgae) could not photosynthesize and would die. Scientists think phytoplankton growth is limited by the amount of iron available in up to one-third of the world's oceans. The North Atlantic's surface water iron levels run five times higher than those of the North Pacific, largely due to North African dust. More iron encourages more phytoplankton growth, which, in turn, feeds more abundant sea life in the North Atlantic. This strong evidence supports the theory that dust serves as a vital ingredient for open ocean food webs and for those that depend on the ocean for food, including humans.

As phytoplankton photosynthesize, they work to slow climate change by absorbing carbon dioxide, a greenhouse gas. They also produce oxygen; in fact, they're responsible for at least half of all oxygen produced on Earth annually. Another surprise—one

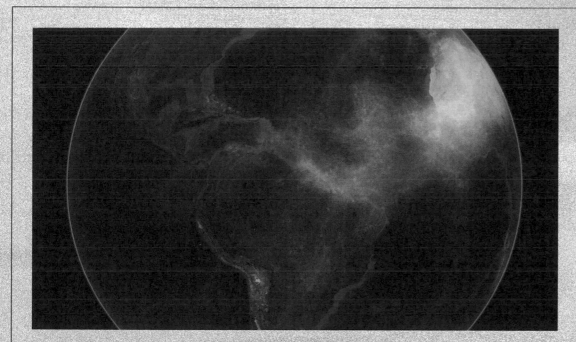

Dust from the Sahel and the Sahara Desert in North Africa makes its way across the Atlantic to the Amazon rainforest in South America.

species of phytoplankton creates more oxygen than all of Earth's rainforests combined! When I consider how miniscule amounts of nutrients, carried by dust, nourish the trillions of tiny phytoplankton that contribute so much to our global ecosystem, I am filled with wonder.

How does NASA measure the river of dust high in the atmosphere?

In 2002, NASA began launching a coordinated series of satellites to study Earth from space. They have captured an enormous amount of information, including data about water in all its forms, airborne particles, vegetation, temperature, air quality and ozone, cloud content and formation, wind velocity, and carbon dioxide levels (a key factor in climate change), as well as phytoplankton growth in the ocean. Data from these satellites have been used in thousands of research papers.

Originally flying together in formation at over 15,000 miles (24,140 kilometres) per hour, this group of satellites was first nicknamed the A-Train, because the leading and trailing satellites had names starting with the letter *A*. Later, the group was also referred to as the Afternoon Constellation, because the satellites circled the globe from pole to pole, crossing the equator at about 1:30 in the afternoon, local time, every day. Two satellites in this group—CALIPSO (a joint mission with the Centre National d'Études Spatiales) and CloudSat, both launched in 2006—were the first to provide the data that help scientists accurately measure the river of dust, using radar and lidar to create three-dimensional pictures. In 2018, NASA placed CALIPSO and CloudSat in a lower orbit; the pair is now called the C-Train. Like other satellites, once they stop working, they'll eventually burn up as they reenter the atmosphere they once observed.

As our body of scientific knowledge grows, researchers, scientists, and engineers work together to continue to improve the tools and technology they use to capture data. The satellites described here reflect only a snapshot in time in the twenty-first century. State-of-the-art satellites will be launched to replace older ones or those that malfunction. New forms of monitoring and data collection will replace outdated methods, all with the intent of better understanding our world, our place within it, and how we can best protect and preserve this planet we call home.

For more information about NASA's Earth-monitoring satellites and an educator's guide, please visit my website, www.jilannehoffmann.com.

CALIPSO's lidar sends out pulses of light that bounce off particles in the atmosphere and back to the satellite, showing where dust is concentrated.

CloudSat

CALIPSO

Aqua

GCOM-W1

OCO-2

Aura

Aura: *atmospheric chemistry*

CloudSat: *clouds*

CALIPSO: *particles suspended in the atmosphere*

Aqua: *water systems, including plankton*

GCOM-W1: *water systems, including wind over the ocean*

OCO-2: *atmospheric carbon dioxide*

How do scientists seek to understand our complex global ecosystem?

We learn more every day about how closely connected Earth's ecosystems are, but more information leads to more questions. Many variables, such as fluctuating ocean temperatures and currents, rainfall, and wind patterns, make it difficult to forecast whether the greenhouse gases that cause climate change will stir up more or less dust and where that dust will end up.

Over the past several years, estimates of the amount of dust making the journey across the Atlantic have varied significantly, indicating just how difficult it is to measure. Adding to the complexity, new research shows that particulate from burning vegetation in southern Africa is also transported across the Atlantic, contributing phosphorus to the Amazon. But that's not all. Indigenous peoples altered some of the Amazon's soil long before European colonization, and natural processes such as erosion from the Andes also contribute nutrients. But how

much? And where? So many variables! So many questions! How much phosphorus is related to human activity? How much is due to dust from the Sahel, and how much from the burning of vegetation? Why does the amount of dust vary? How do rain and wind patterns change dust distribution? How will climate change affect all these variables? Right now, scientists are working to answer these and many other questions.

Scientists use computer models that process large quantities of data from many sources to predict how changes to one system will affect others. Some models suggest that the Sahel will become drier in the future, while others predict the opposite. If the drought predictions are correct, increased levels of dust could block sunlight that would otherwise warm the ocean, resulting in cooler sea temperatures that suppress Atlantic hurricanes. High levels of dust carried aloft by hot, dry winds would also tend to break up tropical waves that can turn into hurricanes. However, if the heavier rainfall predictions are correct, there will be less dust, which would have the opposite effect.

How do scientists respond to these uncertainties? Do they throw up their hands and give up? No! They seek out and share information across scientific fields that will help improve the accuracy of their predictions. Oceanographers, marine biologists, engineers, atmospheric scientists, physicists, and many others are all joining forces to understand the impact that greenhouse gases are having on climate change around the world. Like the specks of dust from the Sahel, scientists are working together to keep Earth a hospitable place for all living beings.

How did South America and Africa drift apart?

Two hundred million years ago, Earth had a single supercontinent called Pangaea that slowly began to break apart into smaller land masses, eventually becoming the seven continents. How do we know? Rocks hold the answer.

The first supporting evidence was presented in the early 1910s. South America, Africa, India, Antarctica, and Australia share similar plant, land reptile, or freshwater reptile fossils. The Appalachian Mountains in the United States contain the same types and ages of rocks found in Greenland and Scotland. In addition, coal deposits and ancient coral reef fossils found in cold-climate areas show that they were once located in the tropics. But even with this evidence, scientists suggested that other explanations were more likely than drifting continents.

In the 1950s, scientists discovered magnetic clues hidden within rocks that gave them the answer. When all the continents were put together like the pieces of a puzzle—snuggling South America into the

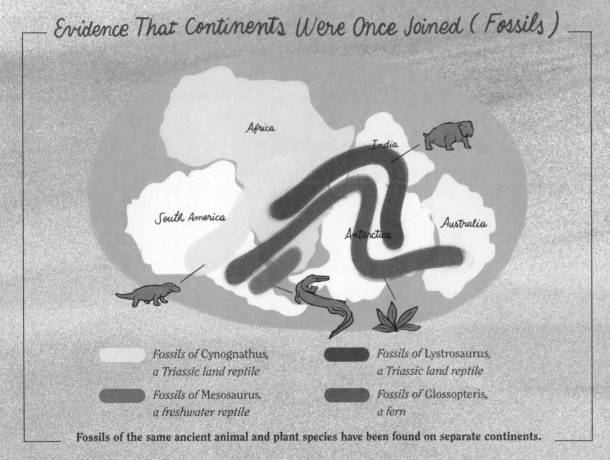

Evidence That Continents Were Once Joined (Fossils)

Africa

India

South America

Antarctica

Australia

Fossils of Cynognathus, a Triassic land reptile

Fossils of Mesosaurus, a freshwater reptile

Fossils of Lystrosaurus, a Triassic land reptile

Fossils of Glossopteris, a fern

Fossils of the same ancient animal and plant species have been found on separate continents.

hollow of Africa, for example—the magnetic minerals in rocks of the same age from each continent all aligned with the same magnetic north pole. The continents had drifted!

We now know that Earth's crust is broken into multiple plates that continue to move very slowly over time, causing earthquakes, raising mountains, cleaving enormous rifts in the crust, and spreading the seafloor. We also know that North America and Europe are moving away from each other at a rate of about 1 inch (2.5 centimetres) per year. At some point in Earth's very distant future, Africa and South America and all the other continents may once again be joined into a single land mass. Scientific models disagree on how they will come together, but they have plenty of time to debate, as this shouldn't happen for another 250 million years.

Evidence That Continents Were Once Joined (Rocks)

North America

Europe

Africa

South America

⬛ Continental shelf

⬜ Matching ancient rock formations

Matching rock formations have been found across the land masses that made up the supercontinent Pangaea 200 million years ago (sections of India, Asia, Australia, and Antarctica are not shown).

Author's Note

When I was in middle school, I learned that dust from North Africa traveled across the Atlantic Ocean to fall on North and South America. This wasn't a lesson in school—it was on the evening news. The idea that dust could travel that far boggled my mind. I had so many questions: *Was it different from the dust that blew across the fields of our farm? How much dust made the entire trip? How much fell into the ocean?* The news report didn't answer any of my questions. So in 2015, when an email from NASA about a "river of dust" landed in my inbox, I took it as a sign that I needed to share NASA's discoveries with others. In the summer of 2020, dust was once again a headline on the evening news, when a plume from the Sahara Desert and its southern border, the Sahel, blanketed the Caribbean and the southeastern United States. This time, I was excited because I knew so much more about it. Through my research, I had learned what North African dust carries, how it varies by season, how it can change weather patterns, and how it affects the Amazon and the deep ocean. I marvel at how these tiny specks from one of the driest parts of the world nourish two of the wettest ecosystems thousands of miles away. And I am inspired by seeing how something so small can make such a big difference.

A book about science is only a snapshot of what was known when it was written. As this book approaches publication, new research suggests that the source of the majority of dust reaching South America may actually come from El Djouf, an area of Mauritania and Mali that lies in the southern Sahara Desert, roughly 1,600 miles (2,570 kilometres) west of the Bodélé Depression. Future research will show whether this new analysis is correct.

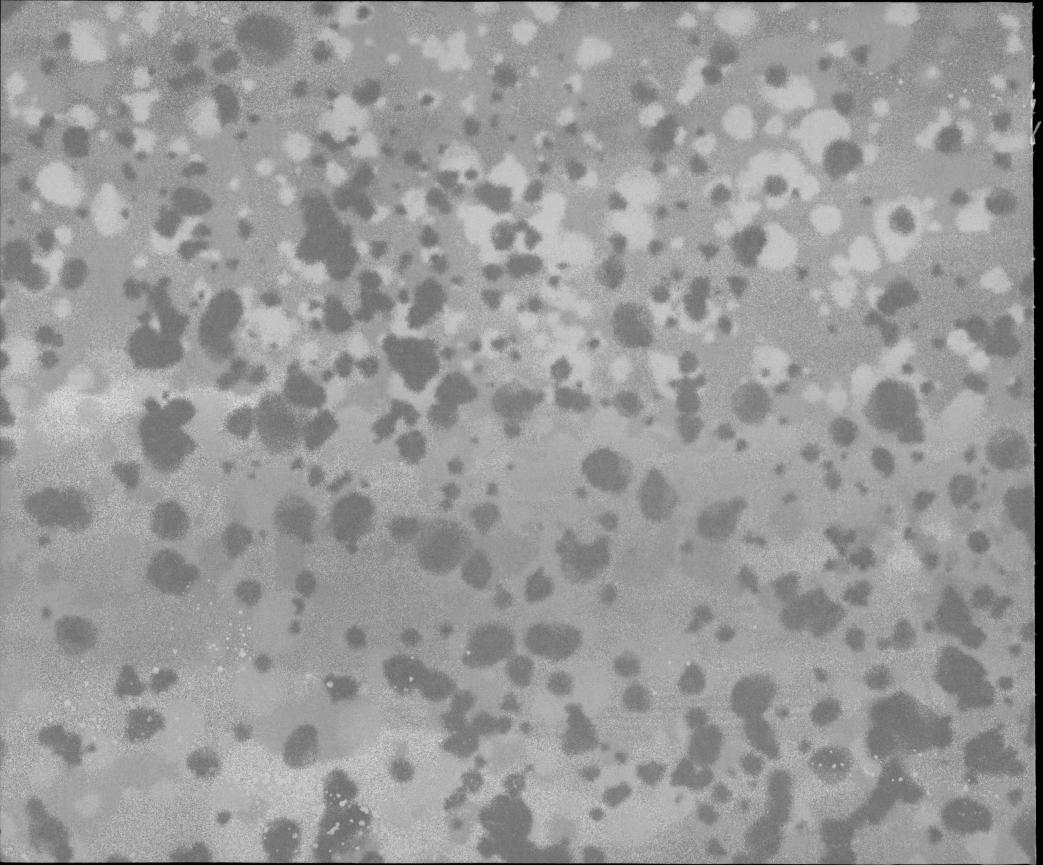